FEUER AND MARTIN

PRESENT

A Musical Fable of Broadway
Based on a story and characters by
DAMON RUNYON

MUSIC AND LYRICS BY
FRANK LOESSER

BOOK BY
JO SWERLING and ABE BURROWS

Staged by GEORGE S. KAUFMAN

Dances and Musical Numbers Staged by MICHAEL KIDD

Settings and Lighting by JO MIELZINER

Musical Director IRVING ACTMAN

VOCAL SCORE

A Publication of
FRANK MUSIC CORP.

Exclusively Distributed by
Hal Leonard Publishing Corporation
7777 West Bluemound Road P.O. Box 13819 Milwaukee, WI 53213

ISBN 0-88188-208-9

NOTICE

Purchase of this vocal score does not entitle the purchaser to perform the work in public. For information regarding performances of the work write to:

The Feuer and Martin production of GUYS AND DOLLS was first presented at the 46th Street Theatre, New York City, on November 24, 1950, with the following cast:

NICELY-NICELY JOHNSON............................STUBBY KAYE

BENNY SOUTHSTREET..............................JOHNNY SILVER

RUSTY CHARLIE....................... ....DOUGLAS DEANE

SARAH BROWN..ISABEL BIGLEY

ARVIDE ABERNATHY...............................PAT ROONEY, SR.

MISSION BAND { ....MARGERY OLDROYD

....PAUL MIGAN

.........................CHRISTINE MATSIOS

HARRY THE HORSE...TOM PEDI

LT. BRANNIGAN...PAUL REED

NATHAN DETROIT......................................SAM LEVENE

ANGIE THE OX......................................TONY GARDELL

MISS ADELAIDE.....................................VIVIAN BLAINE

SKY MASTERSON.....................................ROBERT ALDA

JOEY BILTMORE..BERN HOFFMAN

MIMI..BEVERLY TASSONI

GENERAL MATILDA B. CARTWRIGHT.................NETTA PACKER

BIG JULE...B. S. PULLY

DRUNK..EDDIE PHILLIPS

WAITER..JOE MALAN

DANCERS AND SINGERS

SCENES

ACT ONE

Scene 1. Broadway.
Scene 2. Interior of the Save-A-Soul Mission.
Scene 3. A Phone Booth.
Scene 4. The Hot Box.
Scene 5. Off Broadway.
Scene 6. Exterior of the Mission. Noon, the next day.
Scene 7. Off Broadway.
Scene 8. Havana, Cuba.
Scene 9. Outside El Cafe Cubana. Immediately following.
Scene 10. Exterior of Mission.

ACT TWO

Scene 1. The Hot Box.
Scene 2. The West Forties.
Scene 3. The Crap Game.
Scene 4. Off Broadway.
Scene 5. Interior of the Save-A-Soul Mission.
Scene 6. Near Times Square.
Scene 7. Broadway.

TABLE OF CONTENTS

ACT ONE

ACT TWO

OVERTURE

By FRANK LOESSER

Broadly flowing

OPENING
"RUNYONLAND"

Quick four

Fast two · Still More Chase

marc.

The TOURISTS exit

BENNY bumps the PUG

rit - ard - an - do

Segue No. 2

TRIO—(Nicely-Nicely Johnson, Benny Southstreet and Rusty Charley)
"FUGUE FOR TINHORNS"

14

№ 3   QUINTET— (Sarah, Arvide, Agatha and Mission Group)

"FOLLOW THE FOLD"

18

SAR: sin-ner and you pray no more Fol - low, fol - low the Fold._____

AGA: sin-ner and you pray no more Fol - low, fol - low the Fold._____

ARV: sin-ner and you pray no more Fol - low, fol - low the Fold._____

CORP: sin-ner and you pray no more Fol - low, fol - low the Fold._____

N⁰ 3ᵃ   EXIT OF SARAH AND THE MISSION BAND

Cue: (SARAH) Open all day and night, with a special prayer meeting next Thursday
(start music at word 'special')

No 4 CONCERTED NUMBER
(Nathan, Nicely, Benny the Greek, Brandy-bottle Bates and the Crapshooters)
"THE OLDEST ESTABLISHED"

Cue: (NATHAN) We've been engaged for fourteen years

24

No. 5

REPRISE
"FOLLOW THE FOLD"

Cue: (SKY) There is a large assortment available

Mission Group (off stage)
Unis.

Nº 6

DUET—(Sarah and Sky)
"I'LL KNOW"

Cue: (SARAH) Don't worry, I'll know

Sarah
For I've im-a-gined ev-'ry bit of him, From his strong mor-al fi-bre to the

wis-dom in his head, To the home-y a-ro-ma of his pipe___ *(A Faster)* **Sky** You have wished yourself a

Scars-dale Gal-a-had___ The break-fast eat-ing Brooks Broth-ers type! **Sarah** *(Spoken)* Yes And

Slow *Cue:* (SARAH) All Figured out
I shall meet him when the time is ripe

I'll

No. 6ᵃ

INTERLUDE
"I'LL KNOW"

No. 6ᵇ

VOCAL FINISH
"I'LL KNOW"

Cue: Sky picks up hat-(and exit)

SAR: fly - by - night Broad-way ro - mance   And till then   I shall

SAR: wait   And till then ____ I'll be strong ____ For I'll

SAR: know   when my love ____ comes a - long. ____

Segue during fade-out

Nº 6c   CHANGE OF SCENE

(Scenes 2 to 3)

Very slow

Fade as Nathan starts to speak on phone

No.7   FANFARE

Cue: (NATHAN) I hope you get stabbed by a Studebaker! *(Blackout)*

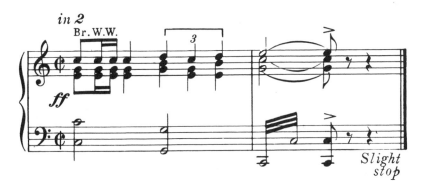

No.7a   SONG and CHORUS– (Miss Adelaide and the Hot-Box Dolls)

"A BUSHEL AND A PECK"

Cue: (MASTER OF CEREMONIES) Miss Adelaide and the Hot-Box Farmerettes!

Slower

Adelaide

I love you a bushel and a peck a bu-shel and a peck And a

hug a-round the neck Hug a-round the neck and a bar-rel and a heap

Bar-rel and a heap and I'm talk-in' in my sleep a-bout you

Chorus

a-bout

a-bout you 'Cause I love you a

you?

(Dolls voices)

My heart is leap-in' Hav-in' trouble sleepin'

Adelaide & Dolls

ADE
bu-shel and a peck you bet your pret-ty neck I do Doo-dle oo-dle oo-dle

Girls
doo-dle oo-dle oo-dle Doo-dle oo-dle oo-dle ooo Goo'-bye now

Bass Drums

(Adelaide & Dolls exit)

Girls
Doo-dle oo-dle oo-dle doo-dle oo-dle oo-dle Doo-dle oo-dle oo-dle ooo

Slow Segue

No. 7b

THE CUSTOMERS EXIT
("HOME, SWEET HOME")

Softly

rit.

Nº 8

SONG—(Adelaide)
"ADELAIDE'S LAMENT"

DUET — (Nicely and Benny)

"GUYS AND DOLLS"

Cue: (NICELY) A world-wide weakness, Look!

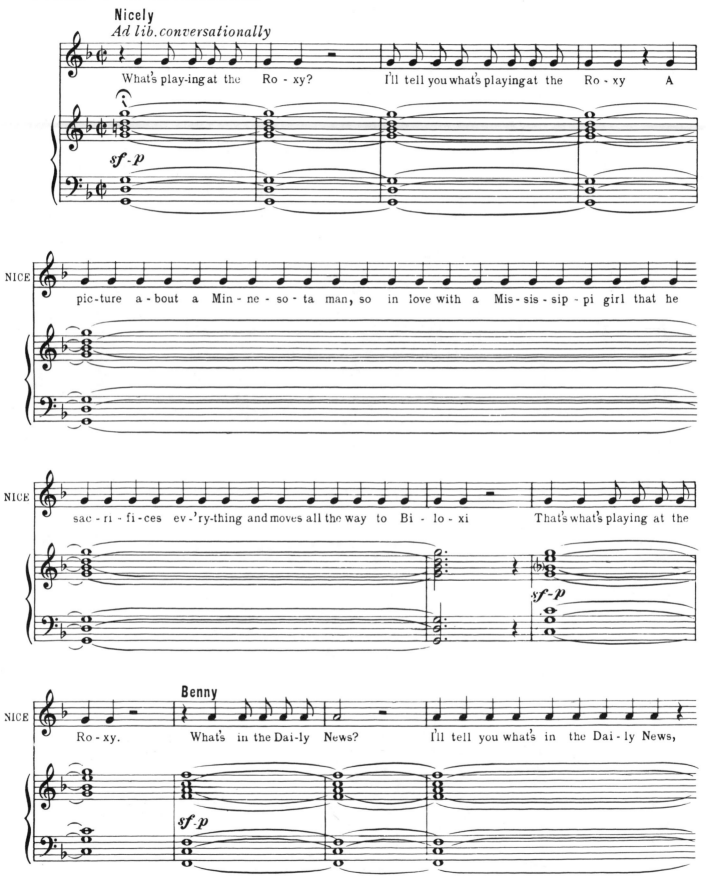

Nicely
Ad lib. conversationally

What's play-ing at the Ro - xy?   I'll tell you what's playing at the Ro - xy   A

pic-ture a-bout a Min - ne - so - ta man, so in love with a Mis - sis - sip - pi girl that he

sac - ri - fi - ces ev - 'ry-thing and moves all the way to Bi - lo - xi   That's what's playing at the

Ro - xy.   **Benny** What's in the Dai-ly News?   I'll tell you what's in the Dai - ly News,

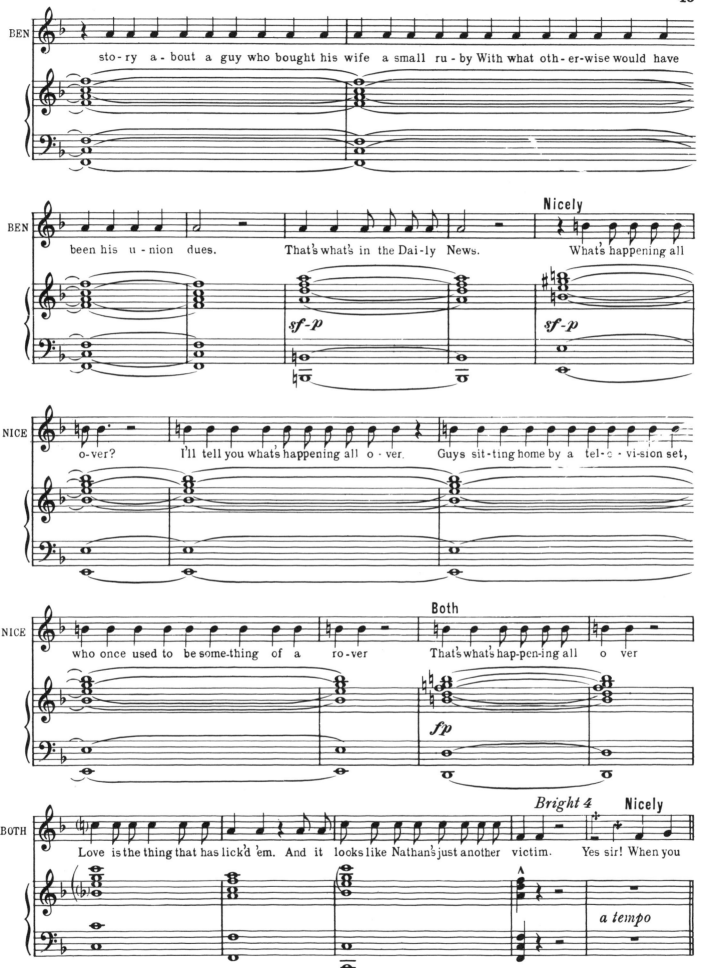

BEN: And he smells from Vi-tal - is and Bar - ba - sol

NICE: Call it dumb, call it clev - er, Ah, but you can give odds for ev - er that the

BEN: Call it dumb, call it clev - er, Ah, but you can give odds for ev - er that the

BOTH: guy's on - ly do-ing it For some doll some doll some doll The guy's on - ly

BOTH: do-ing it for some doll.

Segue

No 11   OPENING–SCENE 6

No 12   CHANGE OF SCENE
(Scenes 6 to 7)

Cue: (**SKY**) Hallelujah!

N⁰ 13

END OF SCENE 7

Cue: (NATHAN) She couldn't have gone!

MISSION BAND *off Stage*
Quick March tempo

N⁰ 14

HAVANA

Bright tempo

SKY and SARAH *enter*

Dialogue in tempo

Sarah

El San-to Cristo, the second oldest Mission in Cu-ba

Sky **Sarah**

Come on! Where to? To see the

SAR old-est

SAR Don't miss the Dungeons where pris'ners were thrown to the sharks. Sounds like a million laughs.

Sky

A la tango

Sarah

These are delicious.

SAR What did you call them? Sky Dul-ce de Leche. Sarah Dul-ce de Leche? What's in it

SAR besides milk? Sky Oh, sug-ar, and a kind of native flavouring. Sarah What's the

The CUBANOS *cross again*

SKY and SARAH *follow*

The CUBANOS *again*

SKY and SARAH *enter*

Fast tempo

The brawl begins

accel.

accel. poco a poco

3 times

ff

SONG– (Sarah)
"IF I WERE A BELL"

Cue: (SARAH) Am I all right?

Slowly

Sarah *Very freely and slightly tipsy*

1. Ask me how do I feel_ Ask me now that we're co-sy and cling-ing_
how do I feel_ From this chem-is-try les-son I'm learn-ing (SKY)(*Spoken*) Chemistry,

Well,sir, all I can say is, If I___ were a bell I'd be ring-ing_
yeah, chemistry. Well,sir, all I can say is, If I___ were a bridge I'd be burn-ing_

_ From the mo-ment we kissed to-night_ That's the way I've just got to be-have_
_ Yes I knew my mor-ale would crack_ From the won-der-ful way that you looked

_ Boy, if I were a lamp I'd light_ And if I___ were a ban-ner I'd wave.
_ Boy, if I were a duck I'd quack_ Or if I___ were a goose I'd be cooked.

SAR

I were a bell — I'd go ding, dong, ding, dong,

SAR

ding.

№ 16

CHANGE OF SCENE
(Scenes 9 to 10)

Cue: (SARAH) You talk just like a missionary

Repeat ad lib. till Curtain

Serenely

Hold till Sarah speaks

SONG– (Sky)
"MY TIME OF DAY"

Cue: (SARAH) She's in love

DUET– (Sky and Sarah)
"I'VE NEVER BEEN IN LOVE BEFORE"

No 18

Cue: (ARVIDE) You're even more tired than I am
(*Whistle cue*)

THE RAID

Very fast and agitated

3rd time pp at BRANNIGAN'S *entrance*

No 19

Cue: (SARAH) I'm a mission doll!

CURTAIN MUSIC

Maestoso

End of Act 1

Nº 20

ENTR'ACTE

Broadly flowing

rall. molto

rit. molto

Direct Segue

Act II

HOT BOX FANFARE

SONG, CHORUS and DANCE— (Adelaide and Dolls)
"TAKE BACK YOUR MINK"

Cue: (MASTER OF CEREMONIES) Miss Adelaide and her Debutantes!

He bought me the fur thing, five win-ters a-go And the

SONG – (Adelaide)

"ADELAIDE'S SECOND LAMENT"

Cue: (SKY) Yeah! *(Exits)* (ADELAIDE *sneezes*)

Adelaide *Freely and sadly*

In oth-er words just from sit-ting a-lone at a ta-ble re-served for two   A

per-son ___ can de-vel-op the   flu   You can   bun-dle her up in her wool-lies And   I mean the

warm-est brand ___ You can   wrap her in sweat-ers and coats 'til it's more than her   frame can stand ___ If she

still gets the feel-ing she's nak-ed, from look-ing at   her   left   hand ___   A

No. 22a

CHANGE OF SCENE
(Scenes 1 to 2)

SONG— (Arvide)

"MORE I CANNOT WISH YOU"

Cue: (ARVIDE) Sarah dear

CHANGE OF SCENE
(Scenes 2 to 3)

Cue: (NICELY) This way!

Agitato

Segue as One 24ᵃ

THE CRAPSHOOTERS' DANCE

Bright tempo

SONG and CHORUS– (Sky and the Crapshooters)
"LUCK BE A LADY"

Cue: (SKY) I've got a little more than dough riding on this one

SKY: might for-get your man-ners, You might re-fuse to stay And

Brightly (*in tempo*)

SKY: so the best that I can do is pray. _____

SKY: Luck be a la - dy to-night. __ Luck be a la - dy to-night. __

SKY: Luck, if you've ev - er been a la - dy to be - gin with —

SKY: Luck be a la - dy to-night. _____

CHANGE OF SCENE
(Scenes 3 to 4)

Bright tempo *(lightly)*

Fade when Big Jule speaks

Nº 27

DUET—(Adelaide and Nathan)

"SUE ME"

Cue: (NATHAN) But I promise you it's true.

Nº 27ª

CHANGE OF SCENE
(Scenes 4 to 5)

SONG and CHORUS—(Nicely)
"SIT DOWN, YOU'RE ROCKIN' THE BOAT"

Cue: (GENERAL) Tell us in your own words

Freely
Nicely

I dreamed last night I got on the boat to Hea-ven And by some chance I had

NICE brought my dice a-long And there I stood And I hol-lered "Someone fade me" But the passengers they know right from

NICE wrong. For the people all said sit down—— Sit down—— you're rock-in' the boat.

Bright - Rhythmic

NICE People all said sit down—— sit down—— you're rockin' the boat—— And the devil will drag you un-

People all said sit down—— sit down—— you're rockin' the boat——

S A
CHO
T B

"THE GUYS FOLLOW THE FOLD"

Cue: (GENERAL) We will now sing № 244 — Follow the Fold

Ens.(unis)

Fol - low the fold and stray no more, stray no more,

ENS stray no more, Put down the bot - tle and we'll say no more

Lights Fade

ENS Fol - low, Fol - low the Fold. _____

Segue
№ 29a

ADELAIDE MEETS SARAH

Nº 30   DUET — (Adelaide and Sarah)

"MARRY THE MAN TODAY"

Cue: (ADELAIDE) What are we, *Crazy* or something?

OPENING—SCENE 7

Bright *in 4*

mf   *sf*   *sf*   *sf*   *sf*

f

pp subito

Fade when Adelaide enters

No 31ª — ENTRANCE OF THE MISSION BAND

Cue: (NICELY) How about the Biltmore Garage?

No 32 — THE HAPPY ENDING

"GUYS AND DOLLS" (All of them)

Cue: (ADELAIDE) Every single night!

ALL spot a John wait-ing out in the rain ____ Chan-ces are he's in-sane as

ALL on-ly a John can be for a Jane ____ When you meet a gent ____ pay-ing

ALL all kinds of rent ____ For a flat that could flat - ten the Taj Ma - hal ____

ALL Call it sad, call it fun - ny, but it's bet-ter than ev - en mon-

molto rall. ff

ALL -ey That the guy's on - ly do-ing it for some doll. ____

Repeat Orch. only for Curtain calls

molto rall.

THAT'S ALL!